D1124575

A Taste
of culture

Foods of
Russia

Titles in the Series

A Taste of Culture

Foods of Russia

Barbara Sheen

KIDHAVEN PRESS
A part of Gale, Cengage Learning

GALE
CENGAGE Learning

Detroit • New York • San Francisco • New Haven, Conn • Waterville, Maine • London

LIBRARY OF CONGRESS CATALOGING-IN-PUBLICATION DATA

Sheen, Barbara.
   Foods of Russia / by Barbara Sheen.
     p. cm. — (Taste of culture)
    Includes bibliographical references and index.
   ISBN 0-7377-3538-4 (hard cover : alk. paper) 1. Cookery, Russian—Juvenile literature. 2. Russia—Social life and customs—Juvenile literature. I. Title. II. Series.
   TX723.3.S447 2006
   641.5947--dc22
                          2006002063

Printed in the United States of America
3 4 5 6 7 12 11 10 09 08

Contents

Chapter 1

Hearty Foods

Russian food is robust and delicious, perfect for satisfying and warming a person during long, cold winters. It depends on grains, mushrooms, and cold-weather vegetables that can withstand Russia's harsh environment.

A Lifesaver

For centuries, grains like wheat and rye have provided the Russian people with the most important part of their diet—bread. Not only do Russians love the taste of bread, during hard times they have depended on it for their survival.

Although Russia is the largest country in the world, much of its land is not suitable for growing food. Therefore, food has often been scarce. Numerous wars fought

Food Regions of Russia

Arctic Ocean

Pacific Ocean

Moscow

Indian Ocean

Sturgeon

Salmon

Herring

Sheep

Dairy

Wheat-growing land

Other cropland

Mostly grazing lands

Vegetables

Fruits

Potatoes

Soybeans

Corn

Rye

Oats

on Russian soil and severe winters compounded the problem.

During hard times, bread was often the only food available. Sharing it kept many people alive, which may be why **khleba** (k-leba), the Russian word for bread means wealth, friendship, and a meal itself.

Dark and Light

Russians make many different types of breads. But rye bread, which is made by combining whole wheat and rye flour, is the most popular. Rye started out as a weed, which Russian farmers unsuccessfully tried to destroy. When severe weather damaged much of the wheat in the nation without harming the rye, desperate Russians used it for flour. By the 11th century, rye bread was a staple part of the Russian diet.

Russian rye breads can be round or rectangular, tan, brown, almost black, or marbled with all three colors running through them. Some are studded with poppy or caraway seeds, and some are made with molasses, which sweetens them. Others begin with a sourdough starter made with yeast and harmless bacteria.

All Russian ryes share a chewy crust, a soft interior, and an earthy aroma that Russians adore. That is probably why the Russian people eat more rye bread than any other people in the world. And, because Russian bread is made without preservatives, bakeries make fresh, hot loaves several times a day. To a Russian, no meal is complete without a thick slice of rye bread slathered with sweet butter. That

More than a Food

Bread holds an important place in Russian life. As far back as the 1600s, laws regulated the size and quality of bread sold in Russia. In the 18th century, if a baker sold a loaf of bread that was smaller than the size required by law, the baker was beaten.

Because bread is so important, it is a part of many ceremonies. For instance, special breads are served at Russian weddings, and when Russians go Christmas caroling, hot rolls are offered to the singers. In the past, when a Russian died, a tiny bread ladder was placed in the coffin to help the soul of the dead person climb to heaven.

Today, Russians honor bread with a museum in Moscow. It is filled with ancient bread-making tools, old recipes, and replicas of different types of bread.

Tourists visiting the Russian countryside enjoy a traditional welcome that includes salt and bread.

may be why an old Russian saying proclaims: "Poor is a dinner lacking bread."[1]

A Part of Russian Life

Making bread is not the only way Russians use wheat and rye. They use the grains to thicken soups and stews

Kasha

Kasha is a tasty grain that can be eaten like rice or pasta. Most supermarkets sell kasha. This recipe uses beef consommé, but chicken consommé or water can be substituted.

Ingredients:
1 cup kasha
2 cups beef consommé
1 egg
2 tablespoons butter
Salt and pepper to taste

Instructions:
1. Boil the consommé, butter, salt, and pepper in a saucepan.
2. While the liquid is cooking, beat the egg in a bowl. Pour in the kasha and stir.
3. Put the kasha in a nonstick skillet. Cook over high heat, stirring often, for about 3 minutes or until the kasha grains are separated.
4. Lower the heat. Add the boiling liquid. Cover the pan. Cook on low heat until the kasha is soft and the liquid is absorbed.

Serves 4

and to make dumplings and pies. And, buckwheat groats, the inner seeds of the grain, are toasted and made into **kasha**, (kah-sha) a robust, cereal-like food with a slightly sweet, nutty flavor and a rich scent.

Kasha has been a staple in Russia ever since migrating tribes from Central Asia brought it there more than a thousand years ago. Russians boil kasha into a porridge that they top with warm milk, sugar, and butter and they eat it for breakfast almost every day. They serve it with meat and fish, much like pasta or rice. They make it into pancakes. They use it in casseroles. They fill dumplings and pies with it. They boil it with fruit. They fry leftover kasha with mushrooms, onions, and butter and top it with sour cream for a delicious main dish. Kasha is so much a part of Russian life that a grain of kasha is put on a baby's lips when he or she is baptized. "A Russian," a proverb says, "cannot be full-fed without kasha." [2]

A Meat Substitute

Kasha is often cooked with mushrooms, another main-stay of Russian cooking. Because meat was often scarce and expensive in the past, Russians substituted mush-rooms, which are flavorful and filling, for meat. And, when they are gathered fresh from forest floors, they are free.

Mushroom hunting is a late summer/early autumn rit-ual in Russia. During that time, Russian forests are full of people filling baskets with mushrooms. Often grandpar-ents and grandchildren go mushroom hunting together. The grandparents teach the children how to distinguish

A Russian woman proudly displays the delicious mushrooms she has picked in the forest.

between poisonous and edible mushrooms. At the same time, they have fun together.

Once the mushrooms are gathered, they are sorted and cleaned. Most are preserved for the winter by canning, pickling, or drying. To dry mushrooms, Russians gather about two dozen mushrooms and tie one to the next, forming a long strand. The strands are placed on a warm, wood-burning stove to dry. The mossy scent of the mushrooms and the fragrance of the wood fill the air.

Once dried, the strands are hung in Russian kitchens. Cooks pluck mushrooms off the hanging strands to add to almost everything. Dried mushrooms are sautéed with noodles and butter or with potatoes and onions. They are minced and made into patties, stuffed into potato skins, dumplings, and pies, mashed and served on toast, and baked in sour cream–topped casseroles. Author Robert Brenner explains: "In Russia the use of mushrooms is universal . . . what a delectable dish they make."[3]

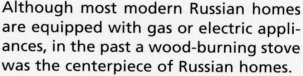

Russian Stoves

Although most modern Russian homes are equipped with gas or electric appliances, in the past a wood-burning stove was the centerpiece of Russian homes. These stoves were huge, taking up about one-fourth of the total living space in a house. They were used not only for cooking, but also to heat the house. The stove was usually built into a corner and was surrounded by benches where adult family members slept. Above the stove was a sleeping loft for the children.

Because it was so prominent, the stove was richly decorated with brightly colored tiles painted with pictures of flowers, animals, and trees. A family's wealth was often measured by the amount of ornamentation on its stove.

Onion

Hearty Vegetables

Hearty vegetables like beets, carrots, radishes, turnips, potatoes, onions, cabbages, and cucumbers, which thrive in Russia's short growing season and can be preserved for winter use, are also vital to the Russian diet. They are the key ingredients in soups, stews, and sauces, as well as serving as appetizers, savory side dishes, and, often, the main course.

Horseradish, a bitter, spicy root vegetable, has a place in almost every garden. Peeled, grated, and combined with sour cream, vinegar, and sugar, it is made into a zesty sauce that Russians use in much the same way as mustard or ketchup.

Beet

Beets, cabbages, onions, and cucumbers are likely to be growing right beside the horseradish. Russians preserve these vegetables by pickling them. Russians have been pickling vegetables since the 9th century, when they learned the skill from Scandinavian tribes that ruled Russia then. Pickled vegetables are served as a side dish at almost every meal, and they are used in cooking just the way fresh and frozen vegetables are used in America. Many Russians still pickle their own vegetables. "Women spend the whole month of September pickling pretty much everything [that] grows in the garden, from cabbage, cucumbers and onion, to tomatoes and watermelon,"[4] explains food writer Sylvia Rector. And Russian markets offer pickled vegetables that shoppers fish out of stout wooden barrels filled with brine.

Pickled, cooked, and raw vegetables are all used in salads. Some salads consist of just one vegetable, such as

A boy seals jars of pickled tomatoes, cucumbers, and other vegetables that will be used to spice up food during the long Russian winter.

Pickled Mushrooms

Here is an easy way to make pickled mushrooms. This recipe uses canned mushrooms. Cooked fresh mushrooms can be substituted.

Ingredients:
1 6-ounce can mushrooms
1 small onion, sliced into thin rings
⅓ cup vegetable oil
⅓ cup red wine vinegar
1 tablespoon brown sugar
1 teaspoon salt
2 teaspoons dill
1 teaspoon mustard

Instructions:
1. Combine all the ingredients except the mushrooms in a saucepan and boil.
2. Drain the mushrooms. Add the mushrooms to the boiling mixture. Cook on low heat for 5 minutes.
3. Put the mixture in a bowl. Cover the bowl and refrigerate for 2 to 3 hours. Drain before serving.

Serves 4

radishes, served with hard-boiled eggs. When the radishes and eggs are topped with sour cream sauce, the many flavors that emerge are a delicious surprise.

Russians also like to mince cooked or pickled vegetables with salt, pepper, and other ingredients to create soft, tasty spreads that they call vegetable caviars. They mince beets, walnuts, prunes, and mayonnaise to create sweet beet caviar. Other vegetable caviars feature eggplant, mushrooms, squash, or beans. These are served in brightly colored little bowls and eaten smeared on slices of chewy rye bread. According to Russian food experts Anya von Bremzen and John Welchman, these delectable spreads are "unfailingly present on every Russian table today."[5]

Russian tables are laden with lots of delicious foods. Although Russia's harsh environment has often limited Russian cooks' choices of available ingredients, by using grains, mushrooms, and hearty vegetables, Russian cooks have created many delectable dishes. These important ingredients are essential to Russian cooking, and in the past, they were central to the survival of the Russian people.

Chapter 2

Wholesome Cooking

The Russian people's favorite foods are wholesome, flavorful, and filling. Although there are regional differences in some of the ingredients Russian cooks favor, thick soups, plump dumplings and pies, and creamy beef Stroganoff are among everyone's favorites. These delicious dishes satisfy even the largest appetites, and they taste sensational.

Nourishing Soups

It is hard to imagine a Russian kitchen without a pot of soup simmering on the stove. Soup has been a favorite of the Russian people for centuries. In fact, more than a dozen varieties of soup were commonly served at a single meal at the palace of the czar during the sixteenth century. These included 50 different varieties of ukha (uk-ha), a fish soup; wild mushroom soup; okroshka (ok-rush-ka), a cold soup made with kvass (k-vas), a fermented liquid similar to beer; **borscht** (borsh-t), a beet soup; and **shchi** (shchee), cabbage soup.

Shchi

This cabbage soup is not difficult to make, but it does use a number of ingredients. This recipe uses ready-made beef consommé in place of homemade stock.

Ingredients:

2 ½ cups cabbage, coarsely shredded
4 14-ounce cans beef consommé
1 carrot, peeled and sliced into
    small pieces
1 medium potato, peeled
    and cut into small chunks
1 celery stalk, sliced
1 tomato, chopped
Salt and pepper to taste

Instructions:

1. Pour the consommé into a large pot.
2. Add the other ingredients. Bring to a boil, reduce heat, and simmer over low heat for about 2 hours. Serve with a spoonful of sour cream, if desired.

Serves 4 to 6

Borscht and shchi are still among the most popular soups in Russia today. In fact, shchi, with its hearty, fresh taste, is often called Russia's national soup.

Every Russian cook has his or her own recipe for shchi. What goes into the pot usually depends on what the cook has on hand. No matter the other ingredients, shchi starts with stock, a broth that is made by slowly cooking meat bones in water. In spring and summer, fresh cabbage is added to the stock. The rest of the year, pickled cabbage (sauerkraut) is used, which gives the soup a saltier taste. Onions, carrots, turnips, and celery add to the flavor. Mushrooms, tomatoes, parsnips, parsley, and dill are other popular ingredients. In the past, when only the wealthy could afford meat, well-to-do cooks added sausage and beef to the soup. Today the addition of meat depends on the cook's preference.

More than Twenty Ingredients

Borscht, which originated in Ukraine, starts out with stock. Instead of cabbage, beets are the primary ingredient. Like shchi, it can contain any number of other ingredients. Some cooks have been known to use more than twenty different ingredients in their borscht. Shredded cabbage, carrots, potatoes, onions, garlic, pepper, ham, pork, and beef all are commonly used. Sugar and a hint of vine-

Filled with chunks of beef and slices of onion and cabbage, a steaming bowl of borscht is a hearty start to any meal.

gar give the soup a sweet yet tart flavor. It is served hot in winter and cold in summer.

Both soups are cooked for hours. This gives the flavors a chance to intermingle. Chef Catherine Cheremeteff Jones recalls her Russian grandmother telling her that "her mother would start cooking [borscht] at six o'clock in the morning. She would cut all the vegetables by hand. . . . Then she left the soup to simmer all day."[6]

After the soups are cooked, they are usually refrigerated overnight, then slowly reheated the next day, which intensifies the flavor. The soups are usually topped with a spoonful of sour cream. The cream thickens the already robust soups and adds a rich, velvety texture and a

A Russian woman stirs a pot of soup that has been simmering on the stove for hours.

creamy, sour taste. The result, according to Russian cooking expert Olga Timokhina "is hearty and filling, chock-full of . . . flavor."[7]

Russian Frozen Food

A first course of borscht or shchi is often followed by a second course of plump, savory dumplings. Russian cooks make lots of different dumplings, but **pelmeni** (pel-meny) is among the most popular. These luscious little half-moons are made of unsweetened dough stuffed with ground pork or beef.

Dumplings like pelmeni came from China and the people of Siberia, the most northerly part of Russia, borrowed the idea. Traditionally cooks made hundreds of the little dumplings, which they froze in the snow. Once frozen, they were stored outside in large sacks. Like modern frozen food, pelmeni could be easily cooked in a pot of boiling water or broth. This transformed the frozen tidbits into hot, tender treats. Cheremeteff Jones describes her friend Antonia's experience: "She used to make pelmeny with her family in Siberia. As they made them, they would throw them out the kitchen window into the snow, to freeze them for later enjoyment."[8]

A Group Activity

Making pelmeni is not easy. The dough, which is made with flour, water, and eggs, must be kneaded and rolled out repeatedly until it is paper-thin. Then the cook cuts little dough circles. Each circle is filled with hot, ground meat and onions, then folded in half.

Cutting, filling, and folding each pelmeni by hand is time-consuming. To simplify the process, some cooks use a special pelmeni mold that allows the cook to make two dozen dumplings at one time.

Even using a mold, making pelmeni is lots of work. To make the job easier, Russians have pelmeni-making parties. At these gatherings, friends and relatives talk, laugh, and sing as they work. When their work is done, they feast on fresh, hot pelmeni topped with melted butter and sour cream. The dumplings taste moist, rich, and tender. "There are few more convenient, spirit warming, filling dishes on a cold winter's day,"[9] explains writer Cheryl Adams Rychkova.

Savory Pies

Pirozhki (pir-o-shki) and **pierogi** (pir-o-gy) are other yummy pastries that are likely to accompany a steaming bowl of soup or be served as a meal by themselves. Pirozhki are miniature pies or tarts, while pierogi are full-sized pies. Both are made with yeast dough and stuffed to bursting with fillings based on ground meat, fish, kasha, mushrooms, cabbage sautéed with onions, hard-boiled eggs, and dill.

A smiling waitress in a countryside restaurant serves a large helping of pelmeni to hungry diners.

Fortune-Telling Pelmeni

In the past, Russian cooks often put coins, hairs, peppercorns, and bits of bread inside pelmeni. These items were used to tell the diner's fortune. For instance, if a diner got a pelmeni with a coin inside it, that meant he or she would become rich. The hair meant the person would have a long life, while the pepper meant that the finder had a bad temper and needed to learn to control it. The bread signified kindness and meant the finder would always be loved.

Although the fillings are delicious, it is the crust, made with whole milk, eggs, and sweet butter, that makes these pies special. Russian cooks pride themselves on their pie crusts. The best, according to von Bremzen and Welchman, are "light as a goose-feather pillow, the crust a golden brown perfection." [10]

The larger pies are baked, while the smaller pies can be baked or deep-fried, depending upon the cook. Once the pie is done, its top crust is rubbed with butter, which keeps it moist. The pies are served warm. The results are so pleasing that Russians and visitors alike find the pies irresistible. *Saveur* magazine editor Margo True describes the cabbage pierogi she ate in a friend's home in Moscow like this: "The pie's buttery sweet filling and rich crust were so satisfying on that frigid afternoon that we ended up having seconds. [It] . . . warmed us from head to toe." [11]

Creamy Beef Stroganoff

Beef Stroganoff is another tasty and warming Russian favorite. It consists of thin slices of steak sautéed in butter with onions and topped with a velvety sauce made with tomato sauce, stock, sour cream, and meat juices. This incredibly rich dish is usually served with mashed potatoes.

The delicious smells of dinner fill a small kitchen in an apartment in St. Petersburg.

Beef Stroganoff

This dish is not hard to make. You can substitute already cooked beef to make the recipe even easier.

Ingredients:

8 ounces egg noodles
1 pound steak or roast beef cut into very thin slices
8 ounces sour cream
4 ounces canned mushrooms, drained
1 tablespoon flour
1 packet onion soup mix
1/3 cup water
1 tablespoon vegetable oil
1 tablespoon butter or margarine

Instructions:

1. Cook the noodles according to the package directions.
2. Heat the oil in a pan. Add the meat. Cook the meat until it is browned.
3. Add the mushrooms, onion soup mix, and water. Cook on low heat for 10 minutes.
4. Sprinkle the flour evenly over the mixture. Add the sour cream. Cook on low heat until the sour cream is warm.
5. Drain the noodles. Add the butter and mix. Serve the beef Stroganoff over the noodles.

Serves 4

Not only does beef Stroganoff have a rich taste, because it is made with the finest cuts of meat, in the past it was a dish that only rich people enjoyed. Historians say beef Stroganoff was created in the late 1800s by a chef working for Count Paul Stroganoff, a Russian aristocrat famed for hosting lavish feasts. According to legend, the count had recently lost his teeth. The chef created beef Stroganoff, which is so tender that it practically melts in the mouth and requires little chewing. It was soon the rage among Russian nobles. And today, when beef is affordable for all Russians, it is popular with everyone.

Delicious dishes like creamy beef Stroganoff, thick, robust shchi and borscht, plump pelmeni, and flaky pirozhki fill and warm a person's stomach and spirit. No wonder they are among Russia's favorite foods.

chapter 3

Tea and Sweets

When Russians want a snack, nothing satisfies them more than a cup of hot tea accompanied by a variety of sweet treats. Other sweet favorites are the perfect way to end a meal.

A Cure for Drowsiness

Russians love tea. They drink it day and night. But when tea first arrived in Russia, it was not as popular. That was in 1638, when the leader of Mongolia sent a package of tea leaves to the czar. The czar did not like the tea's bitter taste, but he liked the way it kept him from falling asleep during long church services. Drinking tea to prevent drowsiness soon became fashionable with Russian nobility. Over time, they came to appreciate its dark flavor.

Because tea was quite expensive, for the next century tea drinking was limited to the wealthy. Serving it was a status symbol among Russian nobles, who threw extravagant tea parties for hundreds of guests. Russian peasants, on the other hand, did not start drinking tea until the early 19th century, when it became affordable.

Two men enjoy their afternoon tea at a traditional tea house in Moscow.

Tea with a Bite

Rather than adding a spoonful of sugar to their tea, many Russians sweeten their tea with sugar cubes. Instead of stirring the sugar cube into their tea, Russians take a small bite of the sugar cube and mix the sugar with the tea in their mouths. This practice is known as "taking tea with a bite."

A Cup of Friendship

Today Russians of all economic backgrounds adore the drink. They sip it at home, at work, in restaurants, in trains, and in little cafés. It is customary for Russians to take two or three tea breaks a day.

Guests know they will be warmly welcomed with a steaming cup and a delicious snack as soon as they walk in the door, because in Russia, sharing a cup of tea is a way to share conversation and friendship. "Everyday life in Russia would be simply unimaginable without the perennial accompaniment of tea," explain von Bremzen and Welchman. "The compact kitchen table is the great gathering place of the Russian people, the scene of endless conversations . . . during which the [tea] kettle never gets a minute off."[12]

Brewing Tea

Russians are very particular about their tea and the way it is brewed and served. Until the early 1900s the traditional way of brewing water for tea in Russia was in a **samovar** (sam-o-var). This is an urn-like device with a spigot in the front that is specially designed to heat and dispense water.

No one knows whether the first samovar came from Persia (the former name for Iran) or Russia. But Russians

An elderly woman enjoys a cup of tea brewed in a samovar at an outdoor market in Moscow.

Apple Sharlotka

Apple sharlotka is easy to make. This recipe uses Granny Smith apples but any tart apple can be used.

Ingredients:
4 medium Granny Smith
    apples, peeled, cored,
    and cut into small
    slices
½ cup sugar
2 eggs
¾ cup flour
unseasoned breadcrumbs, enough to cover
    the bottom of a 9-inch pan

Instructions:
1. Preheat oven to 350°F.
2. Spray pan with nonstick cooking spray.
3. Cover the bottom of the pan with a thin layer of breadcrumbs.
4. Add the apples.
5. Combine the sugar, eggs, and flour and mix well. Pour evenly over the apples.
6. Bake about 50 minutes or until the top is golden.

Serves 4

started using samovars in the early 1800s. These were made of copper or brass. Some were gold-plated or silver-plated and treated like works of art. They could be as large as 2 feet (0.61m) tall, with separate compartments for boiling eggs. Although samovars are rarely used to-day, many Russians own samovars that have been in their families for years. These hold a place of honor in their homes. They are, according to Cheremeteff Jones, "reminders of the essential place of tea in Russian life." [13]

Into the Teapot

Since samovars are mainly for show in modern Russian homes, most modern Russians boil water in a metal teakettle on the stove. When the water is ready, it is poured into a teapot along with one heaping spoonful of black tea per person, plus a spoonful for the pot. A **tea cozy**, a cloth similar to a potholder, which is often shaped to look like a doll with a full skirt, covers the teapot and keeps it warm while the tea steeps. When the tea is ready, teacups sitting in dainty saucers are filled with half a cup of the brewed tea, and half a cup of steaming water. Sugar cubes and little bowls of fruit preserves, which Russians like to eat with their tea, are placed on the table.

The tea is hot and fragrant. One cup is rarely enough. But there is always more water boiling in the teakettle and plenty of delicious tea for everyone.

Tea Cakes

A gleaming tray piled high with a wide variety of pastries known as tea cakes almost always accompanies tea. There are crispy twigs, sugary snowballs, melt-in-your-mouth butter cookies, fruit-filled pies, and delicious apple treats, to just name a few.

Twigs are tasty little cookies that are deep-fried rather than baked. Less than an inch (2.5cm) wide, these crispy pastries are often twisted together in a bow, then fried in hot oil. When they are golden brown, they are plucked from the pan and dusted with sugar. Sweet and crunchy, they look like bits of kindling glistening with fresh fallen snow.

Snowballs also resemble their name. These round, crumbly cookies combine butter, sugar, vanilla, flour, and finely chopped nuts. They are baked until they are lightly browned. Then, while they are still warm, they are rolled in powdered sugar until they are snow-white. Sweet and delicate tasting, they are the perfect accompaniment to strong, dark tea.

Apple treats made from crisp tart apples go well with tea. Apples grow in Russia's cool climate, and the Russian

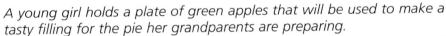

A young girl holds a plate of green apples that will be used to make a tasty filling for the pie her grandparents are preparing.

Snowballs

Snowballs are not difficult to make. This recipe uses pecans, but walnuts or mixed nuts can be used.

Ingredients:
1 cup butter
1 cup powdered sugar, divided
2 cups flour
1 teaspoon vanilla extract
½ teaspoon salt
1 cup chopped pecans

Instructions:
1. Combine the butter and ½ cup sugar together and mix until it is creamy.
2. Add the flour, salt, vanilla, and nuts and mix.
3. Cover the dough. Put it in the refrigerator and chill it for 45 minutes to 1 hour.
4. Remove the dough from the refrigerator. Heat the oven to 350°F. Shape the dough into 1-inch balls.
5. Place the balls on a greased cookie sheet. Bake for about 15 minutes or until the cookies are light brown.
6. Roll the warm cookies in the remaining ½ cup sugar.

Makes about 4 dozen snowballs

people have enjoyed their delicious taste for centuries. Popular apple treats include Russian style apple pies and apple **sharlotka** (shar-lot-ka). Apple sharlotka is similar to an apple crisp. Because it is easy to make and uses ingredients found in most kitchens it is often served to

Russian Hospitality

Russians pride themselves on their hospitality. Guests are always welcome in Russian homes, and it is acceptable to drop in unexpectedly. All visitors are immediately offered tea and food.

Russians are famous for the quantity of food they serve guests. For instance, if there are six guests in a Russian home, the host or hostess usually serves enough food for twelve. A Russian would be terribly upset if a visitor went away hungry.

No guest could possibly go away hungry from this Russian family's table.

guests who arrive without notice. In fact, apple sharlotka is nicknamed "guests at the door" in Russia. To make it, slices of fresh uncooked apples are placed on a layer of bread crumbs. The apples are topped with a batter made from eggs, flour, and sugar. Then the whole thing is baked until it is crisp and golden.

Russian style pies are more difficult to prepare. Like all pierogi, Russian apple pies are made with flaky yeast dough. The filling is made with tart apples or with apple jam. If fresh apples are used, they are peeled, sliced, and cooked with sugar. Then they are placed between two layers of yeast dough and baked until the crust is golden. The result is sweet, but not too sweet. Catherine Cheremeteff Jones says they taste like "a wonderfully delicate apple sandwich that is a special treat for . . . tea."[14]

Fruit Treat

Kisel (kis-el), a yummy custard, is a favorite Russian dessert. Kisel is made with cooked fruit, potato starch, sugar, vanilla, and water. Russians have a number of different recipes for kisel. It can be almost as runny as soup or as dense as jello. This depends on the cook and how much water and potato starch are used.

The cook can also change the texture of kisel by substituting milk for water. Milk gives kisel a velvety texture and a creamy taste similar to homemade pudding. Kisel can be made with almost any fruit. But sour fruits such as cranberries, raspberries, strawberries, and rhubarb are among the most popular.

To make kisel, the fruit is cooked in boiling water until it becomes soft. Then the excess water is strained out. The other ingredients are added, and it is cooked until it thickens. The hot treat is spooned into parfait cups and served hot in winter and cold in summer. Before the custard is served, it may be topped with milk or cream. It looks and smells almost as refreshing as it tastes, and it is a wonderful way to end a meal.

Indeed, a steaming cup of tea accompanied by sweet tea cakes or a delicious bowl of kisel is hard to resist. It is no wonder that when Russians want a snack or a flavorful dessert, these are among their favorite choices.

Food for Celebrations

Russians love to get together and celebrate. Parties and festive events begin with a wide array of hot and cold appetizers known as **zakuski** (za-ku-ski). Other traditional dishes are served only on specific occasions.

Zakuski

Whenever Russians celebrate, the first course is zakuski. Zakuski is a pre-meal spread made up of dozens of hot and cold dishes served **buffet** (buh-fay) style. The food is laid out before the guests arrive, and diners help themselves to whatever they prefer. Rather than eating standing up, as is the custom at many buffets,

Russian Cucumbers

This is an easy dish that is likely to be part of a za-kuski spread.

Ingredients:

3 medium cucumbers
1 teaspoon salt
1 tablespoon lemon juice
⅛ cup dill
1 cup sour cream
Pepper to taste

Instructions:

1. Wash and peel the cucumbers.
   Slice them in thin rounds and sprinkle with salt.
2. Put the cucumbers in a strainer and let them drain for about 1 hour.
3. Put the cucumbers in a bowl. Combine the sour cream, lemon juice, dill, and pepper. Pour the mixture over the cucumbers and mix.
4. Chill for at least 1 hour.

Serves 4 to 6

zakuski eaters sit around the table. This makes it easier for conversation to flow and adds to the fun.

Russians have been enjoying zakuski since the 9th century, when Viking tribes brought the custom, which they called smorgasbord, to Russia. Serving zakuski before a meal quickly became a way to ensure that hungry and tired guests who traveled long distances by carriages and sleds were greeted with food as soon as they reached their destination.

By the 19th century, zakuski spreads had become so extravagant that often more than 50 dishes were served. Typical dishes included hard-boiled eggs stuffed with chopped liver, smoked fish, herring in sour cream sauce, cured meats, bread and sweet butter, pickled vegetables, jellied meats, and fried kasha. These same dishes are still likely to be served today, as are a variety of salads, casseroles, and dumplings. Irina, a Russian woman who authors a Web site dedicated to Russian life and culture, explains: "By the time you have tried everything you will be feeling very full—only to discover that these were only the starters, and that the proper lunch is still to come."[15]

Fishery workers pull eggs that will be made into caviar out of a sturgeon's stomach.

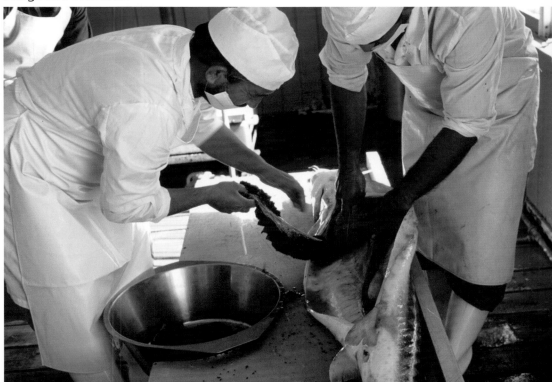

Golden caviar is an extremely expensive treat. The small amount pictured here can cost as much as $200!

Caviar

Among the dozens of zakuski offerings, on very special occasions, there is likely to be caviar. Caviar is the salted eggs or roe of salmon or sturgeon, a large, cold-water fish. It is one of the most expensive foods in the world, costing as much as $200 per ounce (28.35g). One reason for this is it can take up to twenty years for a sturgeon to mature and produce roe. That is why most Russians use caviar from salmon. Although costly, it is not as high priced as caviar from sturgeon.

Despite the expense, on very important occasions, the zakuski table usually has one small crystal bowl filled with caviar. The tiny eggs can be black, gray, or golden if they were harvested from sturgeon, or an orange-red, if they came from salmon.

Guests dab a bit of caviar on a little piece of untoasted white bread. When diners bite into the tiny eggs, the eggs pop open and release oil that tastes buttery smooth and

Cabbage with Apples

Russians love cabbage. Cabbage with apples is a popular zakuski offering.

Ingredients:
1 small white cabbage, with the core and outer leaves removed
1 apple, peeled and coarsely grated
3 tablespoons mayonnaise or sour cream
Salt and pepper to taste

Instructions:
1. Cut the cabbage into 4 parts and then slice thinly.
2. Add the apple, salt, pepper, and mayonnaise or sour cream. Mix well.

Serves 4

slightly salty. Not unlike, according to experts at Russ and Daughters, two New York City caviar dealers, "having the sea kiss your tongue." [16]

Little Suns

While caviar and zakuski are a part of almost every special occasion, other festive dishes appear less frequently.

Blini are topped with a variety of ingredients and can be eaten for breakfast, lunch, or dinner.

Light-as-a-feather pancakes called **blini** (bleen-y), for example, are traditionally served during butter week. That week, which is known as carnival week in other parts of the world, occurs right before Lent, a 40-day period prior to Easter in which many Russians give up meat and dairy for religious reasons.

Butter week was originally an ancient Russian spring festival. Eating round, yellow blini symbolized the arrival of the sun after a cold, dark winter. Once Russians began observing Easter, eating blini became a way to enjoy butter on a grand scale before giving it up for Lent.

It Takes Practice

To make blini, cooks make a batter of flour, butter, water, milk, sugar, eggs, and yeast. The yeast gives blini their delicate taste and texture.

Before the batter is ready to fry, the cook lets it rise two or three times, which adds to its airiness. When the batter is finally ready, the cook greases a cast-iron frying pan with half of a potato dipped in oil. There is just enough oil in the pan to keep the blini from sticking, but not enough for the blini to taste greasy.

When the pan is hot, the cook pours in just the right amount of batter and immediately tilts the pan. This prevents the batter from pooling up, which is essential, since the best blini are the thinnest. In fact, a Russian cook's skill is often measured by the thinness of his or her blini.

Creating perfect blini takes practice. But since cooks usually make dozens at a time, after making the first few,

Easter Eggs

Eggs, which represent rebirth, are an important symbol of Russian Easter. Brightly painted Easter eggs decorate the Easter table. At the end of the meal, it is traditional for the diners to have an egg fight. Each takes an egg and cracks it against his or her neighbor's egg.

Some Easter eggs are not used in egg fights. These are intricately painted. Egg painting is an art form in Russia, and Russian Easter eggs painted to look like dolls or decorated with pictures of flowers and birds are famous throughout the world.

Just as famous are Fabergé eggs. These are enamel eggs decorated with gold and jewels, which were made for the czar.

Painted Easter eggs like these are a traditional art form in Russia.

the whole process gets easier. During butter week Russians eat blini slathered with hot butter and rolled around various fillings such as caviar, smoked fish, or herring, for breakfast, lunch, and dinner. Many people throw blini parties. Sometimes these parties lead to blini eating contests in which Russians stuff themselves on the plump, buttery pancakes. Cheremeteff Jones explains: "A Russian hostess usually allows about ten bliny for each guest. . . . Should a bliny eating contest develop, however, bliny consumption can increase to 25 or even 35 per person."[17] With their light, delicate flavor, it is no wonder Russians cannot get enough of this butter week treat.

An Orthodox priest blesses cakes and hard boiled eggs for Easter.

Symbols of Easter

Once Easter arrives, Russians once again celebrate with food. The Easter feast begins at midnight and goes on, in shifts, all day long. It is a lavish meal that is likely to include zakuski, followed by borscht, pierogi, roast goose, cabbage salad, bread, and cakes. And, although the menu may vary from house to house, two foods, **kulich** (ku-lich) and **paskha** (pask-ha), grace every table.

A table of Russian Orthodox priests enjoys a traditional Easter meal in the company of two lay persons.

Kulich is a tall, sweet bread, shaped like an onion-domed Russian church; while paskha, which literally means "Easter" in Russian, is a sweet and creamy cheese pyramid that Russians spread on kulich. They are served only once a year, on Easter Sunday, and are usually blessed in church the day before the holiday.

Russians have been making these treats for centuries. Many cooks use kulich recipes that have been passed down in their families for generations. Making the cylindrical cake is hard work. Like blini, kulich is made with yeast dough. It can contain as many as 30 eggs and a pound (2.5kg) of butter.

"A proper kulich," according to von Bremzen and Welchman, "should be sinfully rich and feather light at the same time."[18] To accomplish this, the dough is hand kneaded and left to rise three times. Each kneading takes at least an hour. Then it is baked in a coffee tin, which gives the cake its unique shape. While the kulich is in the oven, everyone in the household remains quiet in order to make sure that the cake does not fall.

Paskha making is also tricky. A combination of cottage cheese, butter, egg yolks, heavy cream, and sugar is poured into a special mold shaped like an upside-down flowerpot and refrigerated until it becomes firm. It takes skill to remove the paskha from the mold without breaking it. Once this is done, the cook draws religious symbols on the paskha with nuts and dried fruit.

Paskha and kulich have formed the centerpiece of the Easter meal in Russia for hundreds of years. The holiday would not be the same without them. These traditional foods, along with blini, give special meaning to the Easter season, while zakuski makes every special event more memorable. It is no wonder these foods are such an important part of Russian celebrations.

Mass (weight)

1 ounce (oz.)	= 28.0 grams (g)
8 ounces	= 224.0 grams
1 pound (lb.) or 16 ounces	= 0.45 kilograms (kg)
2.2 pounds	= 1.0 kilogram

Liquid Volume

1 teaspoon (tsp.)	= 5.0 milliliters (ml)
1 tablespoon (tbsp.)	= 15.0 milliliters
1 fluid ounce (oz.)	= 30.0 milliliters
1 cup (c.)	= 240 milliliters
1 pint (pt.)	= 480 milliliters
1 quart (qt.)	= 0.95 liters (l)
1 gallon (gal.)	= 3.80 liters

Pan Sizes

8-inch cake pan	= 20 x 4-centimeter cake pan
9-inch cake pan	= 23 x 3.5-centimeter cake pan
11 x 7-inch baking pan	= 28 x 18-centimeter baking pan
13 x 9-inch baking pan	= 32.5 x 23-centimeter baking pan
9 x 5-inch loaf pan	= 23 x 13-centimeter loaf pan
2-quart casserole	= 2-liter casserole

Length

$\frac{1}{4}$ inch (in.)	= 0.6 centimeters (cm)
$\frac{1}{2}$ inch	= 1.25 centimeters
1 inch	= 2.5 centimeters

Temperature

212° F	= 100° C (boiling point of water)
225° F	= 110° C
250° F	= 120° C
275° F	= 135° C
300° F	= 150° C
325° F	= 160° C
350° F	= 180° C
375° F	= 190° C
400° F	= 200° C

Notes

Chapter 1: Hearty Foods

1. Musya Glants and Joyce Toomre, *Food in Russian History and Culture.* Bloomington: Indiana University Press, 1997, p. 4.

2. Quoted in Olga Timokhina, "Kasha in Russia," RusCusine.com. www.ruscuisine.com/articles/index.php?article=16.

3. Quoted in Anya von Bremzen and John Welchman, *Please to the Table: The Russian Cookbook.* New York: Workman, 1990, p. xxiv.

4. Sylvia Rector, "A Taste of Russia," RusCuisine.com. www.ruscuisine.com/recipes-by-email/archive/030630.html.

5. Von Bremzen and Welchman, *Please to the Table,* p. 16.

Chapter 2: Wholesome Cooking

6. Catherine Cheremeteff Jones, *A Year of Russian Feasts.* Bethesda, MD: Jellyroll, 2002, p. 25.

7. Olga Timokhina, "Russian Schi," RusCuisine.com. www.ruscuisine.com/recipes-by-email/archive/030630.html.

8. Cheremeteff Jones, *A Year of Russian Feasts,* p. 165.

9. Cheryl Adams Rychkova, "The Temptations of Pelmeni," RusCuisine.com. www.ruscuisine.com/articles/index.php?article=34.

10. Von Bremzen and Welchman, *Please to the Table,* p. 451.

11. Margo True, "Russian Hospitality," *Saveur,* December 2005, p. 100.

Chapter 3: Tea and Sweets

12. Von Bremzen and Welchman, *Please to the Table,* p. 546.

13. Cheremeteff Jones, *A Year of Russian Feasts,* p. 75.

14. Cheremeteff Jones, *A Year of Russian Feasts,* p. 80.

Chapter 4: Food for Celebrations

15. Quoted in Cheremeteff Jones, *A Year of Russian Feasts,* p. 80.

16. Russ and Daughters, "Caviar." www.russanddaughters.com/pr_caviar.html.

17. Cheremeteff Jones, *A Year of Russian Feasts,* p. 37.

18. Von Bremzen and Welchman, *Please to the Table,* p. 516.

Glossary

blini: Thin pancakes.

borscht: A beet soup.

buffet: A meal in which food is set out on a table and diners serve themselves.

kasha: A cereal-like food made from the inner seed of buckwheat grain.

khleba: Bread.

kisel: A fruit custard.

kulich: A tall, dome-topped, sweet bread served on Easter.

paskha: A sweet cheese pyramid, which is spread on kulich.

pelmeni: Small, filled dumplings.

pierogi: Sweet and savory pies.

pirozhki: Miniature pies or tarts.

samovar: A device used to boil water.

sharlotka: An apple dessert.

shchi: A cabbage soup.

tea cozy: A cloth similar to a pot holder that is placed over a teapot to keep it warm.

zakuski: A pre-dinner spread of different appetizers.

For Further Exploration

Books

Alla Danishevsky, *Tastes and Tales from Russia*. Baltimore, MD: PublishAmerica, 2004. An adult book filled with recipes and Russian folk tales.

Editorial and Art Department of World Book Publishing, *Christmas in Russia*. Chicago: World Book, 2001. The books talks about how Christmas is celebrated in Russia, with recipes and crafts.

Greg Nickles, *Russia: The Culture*. New York: Crabtree, 2000. Discusses different aspects of daily life in Russia, including holidays, schools, and food.

Gregory Plotkin and Rita Plotkin, *Cooking the Russian Way*. Minneapolis, MN: Lerner, 2002. A Russian cookbook for kids.

Sue Townsend, *Russia*. Chicago: Heinemann Library, 2003. A Russian cookbook for kids.

Web Sites

Explore the World: Russia, Peace Corps KidsWorld (www.peacecorps.gov/kids/world/europemed/russia.html). Gives facts about Russia, including Russian foods and a discussion of how kids live in Russia.

Kids from Russia, Fact Monster (www.factmonster.com/ipka/A0930073.html). Information about family, food, popular games, school, and holidays.

RusCuisine.com (www.ruscuisine.com). Although this Web site is geared toward adults, it is filled with interesting recipes and information about Russia, including links to shopping for items like Russian dolls.

Russia, CIA World Fact Book (www.cia.gov/cia/publications/factbook/geos/rs.html). Gives a map and facts about Russia's geography, economics, and government.

Index

Picture Credits

Cover: Simon Richmond/Lonely Planet Images
AFP/Getty Images, 33
Amana Images/Getty Images, 32
AP Photos, 49
© David Cumming; Eye Ubiquitous/CORBIS, 15
© David Turnley/CORBIS, 36
© Dean Conger/CORBIS, 25, 38, 48
ITAR-TASS/Vladimir Smirnov/Landov, 12
Joseph Paris, 10, 34 (bottom), 42
© Kaveh Kazemi/CORBIS, 43
© Peter Turnley/CORBIS, 22-23, 31
PhotoDisc, 16, 19, 20, 34 (top)
Photos.com, 14
© Rick Barrentine/CORBIS, 37
© Steve Raymer/CORBIS, 27
StockFood/Getty Images, 21, 28, 44, 46
© SYGMA/CORBIS, 50
Tamia Dowlatabadi, 7
© Wolfgang Kaehler/CORBIS, 9

About the Author

Barbara Sheen is the author of numerous works of fiction and nonfiction for young people. She lives in New Mexico with her family. In her spare time, she likes to swim, walk, garden, and read. Of course, she loves to cook!